Panya Banjoko is a UK based writer, poet and a PhD candidate at Nottingham Trent University with a Vice Chancellor awarded scholarship writing a practice-led PhD rooted in Nottingham Black Archive. Her debut collection, Some Things, was published by Burning Eye Books (2018). Her work is published in numerous anthologies including award-winning Clever Girls, winner of the Working-Class Studies Association's 'Jake Ryan and Charles Sackrey Award for a Book about the Working-Class Academic Experience' (London: Palgrave Macmillan, 2019), and her poem, 'They and Them', featured in Mic Drop, an exhibition by artist Keith Piper at the Beaconsfield Gallery in London, the London Film Festival and the International Film Festival Rotterdam. She has been artist in residence at the International School in Stuttgart, Jaipur Literature Festival in India, and for the National Justice Museum in Nottingham. Panya is a multi-award-winning poet, co-ordinates a Black Writers Network and is patron for Nottingham UNESCO City of Literature

(Re)Framing the Archive

Panya Banjoko

Burning Eye

BurningEyeBooks
Never Knowingly
Mainstream

Copyright © 2022 Panya Banjoko

The author asserts the moral right under the Copyright, Designs and Patents Act 1988 to be identified as the author of this work.

All rights reserved. No part of this publication may be reproduced, stored in a retrieval system, or transmitted, in any form or by any means without the prior written consent of the author, nor be otherwise circulated in any form of binding or cover other than that in which it is published and without a similar condition being imposed on the subsequent purchaser.

This edition published by Burning Eye Books 2022

www.burningeye.co.uk

@burningeyebooks

Burning Eye Books
15 West Hill, Portishead, BS20 6LG

ISBN 978-1-913958-27-5

CONTENTS

Stewing	9
Over and Over Again	10
What Must Be Done	13
Making Way	14
Breaking Point	15
Remnants	16
Strong Hold	17
Perusing a Museum	18
Mahogany Abbey	19
After the Lion Hunt	20
River Webb Lualaba	22
Empire's Guardian	23
Corpulent Pigs	24
Lady Velleity	25
Breaking Rank	26
Bystanders	27
Hope	28

STEWING

First, slice ideas from our heads.
Then scold us for being radical.
But watch as we continue to simmer
for the next generation.

OVER AND OVER AGAIN

There was me, and the younger
with the Good Man Prophet
sitting around a table
in the museum café,
breaking our thoughts into segments
we could share.

We were rammed into a corner
shielding ourselves from the stares;
only clinking teaspoons
broke the silence.

The Good Man Prophet's
eyes roamed around the space
seeking out danger, watching for
a flick of a blade, a stray boot.

And the Younger
was sharpening her teeth,
waiting to take chunks out of their hands,
leaving me to mark time
with a pen,

scratch, scratch, scratching,
head down, silently chanting,
Babylon mus' fall.

I recorded the welts on the back of a girl
not more than six,
scratch, scratch, scratching.

The fear of a serviceman,
first time on guard duty,
muddy boots wedged in the trench,

seven-pound rifle
braced on his shoulder;
head down, over the book I pore.

I bite my tongue
for the boy without a mother,
fixed his broken jaw with my pen,

chanting burn bag-o'-wire
for the dozens of heads
bashed against walls,

hands tied behind backs,
beaten and floored.

The Younger,
in step to the beat,
soaked up tales
of forgotten soldiers
superseded by stooges.

After, we slid past the grumbling guard
who defended the gate.

After, our cameras clicked to remind us
of the absence of our fame
as we travelled through galleries

we met the Curator, scraggy-haired,
spectacles hanging from his nose,
sitting behind a desk,

with more than 400 years of melancholy
hanging in the air.

In his grand storeroom
portraits of tell-tales hung,
among files stacked to the ceiling
filled with the great hosts' adventures
and mounds of books

piled on top of one another
and things, like paraffin lamps
and Dutch pots, colonised by dust,
thick and spongy, like moss
burgeoning,

until it all spilled onto the floor
and occupied the perimeter.

Between layers of grimy photographs
abandoned in a box,
his fingers searched out sepia prints
carrying ambitions
from over 4,000 miles away.

Forged on the back were
words filled with hope:
In 5 years we shall return.

He bound them all with bundles of tape
and shoved them towards the back
of a cupboard, then smiled,
knowing the absence of others
is what makes Britian great.

WHAT MUST BE DONE

In this age of preaching over coffins
and listening to sermons of
Dear Lord, do not forget us,
keep us eating cornmeal dumplin' –
maybe a rebellion, or two,
way out on the other side of I'm sick and tired,
beyond vanloads of blaming the Blacks,
is what we hunger.

Away from wagging fingers
telling us what to do
and how we should do it,

there must be more than
staggering to assemble ourselves
around the gilded monuments
we are taught to love.

For now, life and its hard pan bucket
digs through us like dirt,
piling us into heaps
as if our lives don't matter.

MAKING WAY

I tried to decide which way to sleep
terror free,
but still caught the worst dream.

It scraped the insides of me
and all the different edges of my soul.

Then carried me on my back,
placed me in a skull-shaped coffin.

Set me in a castle
piled with rundown hearts
barely beating.

This wild thunder of a dream
repeated itself,
snarling and ripping at my torso,
then hitching me to barbed wire
leaving me to collide with hope.

When morning comes
the words *go forth and collect*
are tattooed on my tongue

BREAKING POINT

Laden with life's grit tacked to her back
and a jar of freshly made courage,
she walks out of the door
with anger creaking in her knees.

Bobbing and ebbing against the rolling tide,
she charts a course through zigzag routes
counting rolling eyes as she storms and swells.

With foghorns' warning she steers
far from the shore
that once anchored her neck.

And as the ocean spills and froths
buffering her between waves,
carrying her pass ship's wrecks
and the flotsam left by unforgiving squalls

she spies a place called Landing
lowers her sails
and discovers her voice.

REMNANTS

It was at the border of the city
where I met the others.

Three days earlier
we brought the castle to the ground

and amongst the ruin
searched for clay to make fluted pots,

decorated them with raised fists,
scored our names along the edges,

then poured our grief into them
until we were light enough to fly.

STRONG HOLD

At best he reminded her of a lament,
at worst
someone who might appear in a line-up.

Lips sealed, he guarded the door,
counting people in
while keeping others out.

He made her tremble.

Clad in an ill-fitting uniform,
this shifty makeshift officer
presided.

Hardened by the charge and thrill
of guarding his stronghold.

But there was nothing inside of the people
who spent two thirds of their lives
building this empire.

Even common strangers agreed.

PERUSING A MUSEUM

Away from the preying eyes of guards
under dim lights in a ducal palace.
We long to trace our fingers
along the contours of one of their finest bronzes.

Admire the artistry:
a statue of a striking man
straight backed, looking down on us
from his plinth of Portland stone,

Walk around its perimeter,
walk around again,
then stand for a moment
wondering how he won the heart of this city.

Taking three steps back
fall into his shadow,
crane necks to see
what an explorer looks like.

Examine every detail:
his rigid glare will hold you.

Up close again,
standing on the tips of toes,
trace the buckles on his dress shoes
with fingers.

Our tongues cannot manage
the word conquistador,
and so, we abandon efforts
to read the gold inscription,

decide instead to count the notches on his belt
to see how many heads he collected
for the city that applauds him year after year.

MAHOGANY ABBEY

In my younger days, I counted more than one hundred pieces
of hardwood furniture spread around the abbey,

large chunks of solid wood sentenced to death
as antique sideboards and cabinets.

Some had reddish-brown sheens to hide their grief,
others had darkened over time with worry.

I half-smiled at their refusal to decay or fade
in this coveted, sinful place.

If beauty has its price, somewhere in the world
homes are flooded with tears lamenting their removal.

So very early in life the lesson began
for what it means to hold power and not to give a damn.

AFTER THE LION HUNT

At the top of every hunter's wish list
is the beast of legends.

Facing it off, on foot,
and shooting straight and quick.

Much later, he records in his book
the days searching green savannahs,

waiting silently
in a boundless wilderness,

hidden behind bush
and acacia trees,

looking down the barrel of his rifle,
staring the beast in the eye,

aiming for where the shoulder joins the neck,
then landing the fatal shot.

Later, his guide would whisper
into a friend's ear:

The beast he called a mankiller
was past its prime

and sagged with bad knees.
Even so, it did not drop

with the first shot
but lay in wait, then charged

at the over-gunned hunter
as he drew closer.

Afterwards, he stands
with his right foot on the beast's head,

rifle held high, and marks himself
the Great White Hunter.

RIVER WEBB LUALABA

To see where chance would take him
and what mischief he could make,
he closed his eyes and placed his pudgy finger on a map.
It landed between a waterfall and marshy lakes,
near a river that bounded and dropped
into a place called the Congo.
He beat his chest in anticipation at the thrill
of penetrating seemingly impassable stretches
and leaving his footprint behind as he renamed each place.

EMPIRE'S GUARDIAN

She is the fifth woman of foolery,
painted with a snake for a tongue
and dressed in a cerulean robe,
with a lion at her side.

Camouflaged by plush,
delicate green foliage,
the axe, held above the lion's head,
is hidden as she sits tall
towering over all.

Sometimes, she is painted with a helmet
and seated with a shield and spear,
but more commonly in the twentieth century,
with the persistence of empires
and the building of states,
she is painted with an eye
on the tip of her snake tongue
to see around corners, watching
and then polishing her version of history.

There are accounts of her being remounted
onto modern card,
smeared with black chalk on white paper,
set against the backdrop
of 1950s colour bar Britain.
Recto: her bold predictions are recorded
after the 2007 bicentenary.
The inscription reads:

WE WILL ALWAYS RULE THE WAVES.

This painting is used as a model in schools.

CORPULENT PIGS

One of a pair, pictured grunting,
poised to swipe.
At the end of each arm is a cudgel.

In the late 1940s fearsome pigs became
barometers of the patriots' success
as they bludgeoned up to fifty settlers per week
at their peak.

Today, they are highly regarded
and displayed in museums in numerous iterations,
often pictured reclining,
with bacon sarnie in hand.

Protected by an impermeable blue border.

LADY VELLEITY

Gilt overlaid (verso) is the painted head
of a middle-aged woman with furrowed brow.
A square hole cut in the vellum
where her mouth was.

She is the compliance regime
popular post-war and for generations thereafter.
Pockmarks are present around the face,
evidence she has been used as a dartboard circa 2007.

Unlike the other portraits in the series,
she has no decorated borders.

But an inscription now partly faded (recto) reads:

Silence is not compliance; it pays the bills.

BREAKING RANK

Go tell the next in line about their grandparents' war,
how they chanted what have you done for us?
Show the records of their standout crimes, reckless acts,
breaking of trust.

Let them hear the clank-clanking of the chains of discord
of those who dodge thick-soled boots
and who riot for freedom's sake. Tell the children
to look back, see if they want a stake.

A nation of mourning mothers with broken frames
and worn hearts, these wrongs are welded together by hate,
then surge when minds are already made up, and councils
commend truth grabbers as their dependable greats.

If you are pleased and proud of hounding the poor,
print it on gold paper,
but know that the act itself
will tip the scale—sooner or later.

BYSTANDERS

The museum was loaded
with Saturday afternoon gawkers
and sticky-fingered kids yapping
at the prospect of ice cream.

Over the sound of swooshing doors
this one bold man curses my skin,
doles out obscenities
as if he's giving out candyfloss
at a summer fair.

Visitors continue browsing display cases,
hunting for the next ahh!
Shushing me for spoiling their roaming
while he drenches me with hate.

I raise my voice and ball my fists
as he lunges towards me –
sometimes you need to jump
in at the deep end, even when
there's no hope of a cushioned fall.

HOPE

If we could soar up and over, then twirl
above the lines of meddling people,
speak our truth and stretch until we unfurl,
purge this world of all its measured evil,
point ourselves towards heavenly retreat
away from those who make us sigh,
shake off their fists which grab like vexing heat,
leap with faith towards the uncluttered sky,
if we could land on green lit by the sun,
defuse the hate that grips and needles deep,
sprinkle this dusty earth when we are done
with monuments for all of us to keep,
if the truth of who we are were not ignored,
there would be no need to bludgeon doors.

ACKNOWLEGEMENT

Thank you to Sharon Monteith.